LET YOUR PROBLEMS TURN YOU INTO A WINNER!

We all have problems that hamper our progress. However, there is a new way of dealing with problems that can turn them into the very break you have been waiting for. *The Opportunity In Every Problem* will open your mind to an awareness of the opportunities you have been missing.

"Great book! It gives you the essential attitude for success and achievement."

—BRIAN TRACY, AUTHOR OF *Victory!*

"*The Opportunity In Every Problem* can open up a new way of looking at and responding to the countless decisions you must make every day in all areas of your life—business, friends, family, and spiritual. Scott Taylor teaches that a true opportunity is anything that benefits you as well as others."

—KEN BLANCHARD, CO-AUTHOR, *The One Minute Manager*®

"**First of all, you have a winner!** While reading this book I found myself changing from a dreamer to a doer. I seldom find material in a book that inspires me to do great things...this one does, and does it well."

—PAUL TULENKO, SYNDICATED SMALL BUSINESS COLUMNIST, *Scripps-Howard News Service*

"This book is for anyone who has had or will have to deal with adversity. While apparently telling a simple, fun and engaging story, Mr. Taylor teaches and inspires us all to reach for the hightest of success by turning the very obstacles that, at first, seem to thwart our efforts, into opportunities. Everyone who wants to succeed in life should read this book."

—HYRUM W. SMITH, VICE CHAIRMAN OF THE BOARD, FranklinCovey

THE OPPORTUNITY
IN EVERY PROBLEM

THE
OPPORTUNITY
IN
EVERY
PROBLEM

by Scott L. Taylor

Gibbs Smith, Publisher
Salt Lake City

First Edition
07 06 05 04 03   5 4 3 2 1

All quotations are borrowed with permission from *Favorite Quotations from
the Collection of Thomas S. Monson* by Thomas S. Monson, pages 131, 132,
133, 135, 147, published by Deseret Book Company, 1985.

Published by
Gibbs Smith, Publisher
P.O. Box 667
Layton, Utah 84041

Orders: (1-800) 748-5439
www.gibbs-smith.com

Edited by Suzanne Gibbs Taylor
Designed and produced by Worksight, New York City
Printed and bound in the United States of America

Library of Congress Cataloging-in-Publication Data
Taylor, Scott, 1964—
    The opportunity in every problem / by Scott Taylor. — 1st ed.
    p. cm.
ISBN 1-58685-320-1
1. Success—Psychological aspects. 2. Problem solving. I. Title.
BF637.S8T285 2003
158.1—dc21

2003000521

Contents

This book is dedicated to my children
Zachary, Lacey, and Cody
who continually give me reasons
to be proud of them and have
kept me smiling amidst
many pressures our family has
endured over recent years.

Foreword

I am happy to be the first to introduce you to "Prolific Thinking," the new thought process developed by Scott L. Taylor and instilled throughout this book. This book is not for the fainthearted. As with all truth that we acquire in life, there is an obligation to act according to the knowledge that we have.

The Opportunity In Every Problem is an engaging story—some may even call it a parable—that clearly extols true principles of success on every level of the human experience. When you read it, you will have to make a choice. You can choose to either apply the principles taught in the book and rise to new levels of success such as you have never seen, or you can choose to think "nice story" and not do anything about what you have learned. Choosing the latter would guarantee that your situation will never improve. However, choosing the former will open the doors to an entirely new life of freedom, success, and happiness.

I thoroughly enjoyed reading *The Opportunity In Every Problem.* I saw myself and many of the people I know in some of the characters portrayed in the story. I believe that there are some people like I. M. Lucky (a sagacious leading character in the story) who instinctively know the principles of success taught in this book, and then there are the rest of us who will recognize its potential once we are taught it. Scott has found a great way to teach us with a simple, fun, and interesting story. He teaches and inspires us all to reach for the heights of success by turning the very obstacles that at first seem to thwart our efforts, into opportunities.

Everyone who wants to succeed in life should read this book. But like I said before, this book is not for the fainthearted. You brave souls who are willing to recognize and change a few erroneous beliefs and attitudes on your "belief window" should get excited about the successes this story is about to develop in your lives.

—HYRUM W. SMITH, CO-FOUNDER, FranklinCovey

Acknowledgements

I would like to offer my most profound gratitude to Amanda Ballif, my mother 'Charli' Hopkins, Kerstin Oquist, and several Samaritan Business Builders members for their assistance.

I express my deepest appreciation to Jennifer Guter of Reflections for designing the first cover of this book and for her many contributions to help small business people succeed.

From the Author

I would first like to thank you for taking the time to open *The Opportunity In Every Problem*. It is my hope that you will utilize the principles for success illustrated within these pages so you can live happier, healthier, and wealthier lives.

I initially had the idea of creating a book to teach people how to turn problems into opportunities for some time. The approach I first contemplated was to write a training manual of sorts, which would give details and structure to a message that really needs to be experienced rather than taught. However, when I finally sat down to write a different book, the thought of *The Opportunity In Every Problem* came to me. As I pondered my dilemma, a rush of inspiration hit me. Without a plan, I started writing. I kept writing for two-and-a-half days until it was completed. Even with several people editing the book, there were minimal changes. A few lines were added for clarification, a few words changed, and several grammatical corrections were made. This book essentially stands as it flowed into my mind. What I am trying to tell you is that this is an inspired work, and I implore you to test these principles to see if you, too, can turn your problems into opportunities.

One word of guidance: You are likely to become excited about turning your problems into opportunities, but please remember that you do not have to do it yourself. The synergy created by involving several people to brainstorm for an opportunity with you will usually give you additional potential for success.

May your life increase in joy, success, and happiness as you apply the principles found in *The Opportunity In Every Problem*.

—SCOTT TAYLOR

CHAPTER 1

Meeting Mr. Lucky

The Man Who Thinks He Can

If you think you are beaten, you are;
If you think you dare not, you don't.
If you like to win, but think you can't,
It's almost a cinch you won't.
If you think you'll lose, you're lost,
For out in the world we find
Success begins with a fellow's will;
It's all in the state of mind.

If you think you're outclassed, you are;
You've got to think high to rise.
You've got to be sure of yourself before
You can ever win a prize.
Life's battles don't always go
To the stronger or faster man;
But soon or late the man who wins
Is the man who thinks he can.

Walter D. Wintle

I n a secluded area of the country on a hill of substantial verdant luster, lived the luckiest man in the world. His surroundings, though seemingly ostentatious, held an enticing romantic lure. There was not a house so big, nor staff so cheerful and content, in all the country. Yet, secrecy and mystery filled the peasants below as they wondered who Mr. I. M. Lucky really was and how he had reached such colossal levels of success.

In a small schoolhouse at the bottom of Lucky Mountain in the village of Dilemmaville, there attended a boy of considerable size yet lacking in self-esteem. The boy's name was Utor Retting, but the local boys and girls knew him only as "Utor the Bore."

Utor tried his hand at sports but was quite

clumsy, and the children made fun of him each time he fell. He was tired of hearing the chant, "He can't make a score 'cause he's Utor the Bore," so he stopped playing sports. He attempted art, but could never appreciate his own work, even though the teacher would tell him he showed promise. He tried to be sociable, but before he could get near a crowd of peers someone would notice him and say, "Look, here comes Utor the Bore!" This would embarrass Utor, causing him to turn and walk away.

One day Utor decided he wasn't going to walk away. He was determined to stay and talk with the group until they finally accepted him. As he approached the crowd of children mocking him with a chant of, "Utor the Bore, can't fit through the door . . . Utor the Bore, can't fit through the door," they expected him to turn and walk away, but this time he stayed there until they stopped chanting. They all stood there staring at each other until "Horace the Brute Force" spoke up and gruffly said, "What do you want?"

Utor responded, "I just want to play with you guys."

Horace reacted in his usual intimidating manner, "Well we don't want to play with you, Utor the Bore. Why don't you just go away before I make you hit the floor, Utor the Bore."

As he turned and walked away with his head drooping, Utor decided right then and there that he was never going to have any friends, so he started looking for something he could do that would provide him a more solitary environment.

Utor loved books and was quite studious, so he thought maybe someday he could be a writer. As his romantic fantasies of sports and art went by the wayside, he began looking for a way to start writing. His teacher encouraged him to start by writing short articles for the school newspaper. Even though this wasn't what Utor was hoping for, he decided he would do whatever was necessary to become a writer.

Utor entered the school news shop only to find the same ridicule. The editor of the school newspaper was incensed to find that Utor the Bore thought he could actually be a writer. In a conspiracy to get Utor to quit, the class came up with an idea that was sure to convince him he was unable to cope with the rigors of school reporting. They thought of the toughest assignment they could give him. This assignment would be impossible. For years the newspaper had tried, with several of their top reporters, to get an interview with Mr. I. M. Lucky, but to no avail.

The editor called Utor into his office and said, "So, Utor, you think you can be a reporter, do you?"

Utor, in a somewhat timid voice said,

"Well, I would like to be a writer."

The editor responded by saying, "A writer! Why, that is an even harder job than being a reporter, but if that's what you want, I'll give you the easiest assignment I can think of to get you started. Heck! If you can't do this assignment then writing is not for you. I want you to get an interview with Mr. Lucky on the hill. Find out how he became so successful and whether I. M. Lucky is his real name."

The thought of having to approach someone as important as Mr. Lucky left Utor with a rather high level of trepidation. However, if this was the easiest assignment he could get, Utor could hardly back down, regardless of his fear.

The next day, Utor went to see Mr. Lucky. As he rode his bicycle up the winding road to the Lucky mansion, he became more and more bewildered over what he would say to Mr. Lucky when they met. At last, he reached the door, winded and nervous. He turned around, looking back at the long distance he traveled to get there. A faint thought of how far he was from the security of his home caused him to reconsider his desire to become a writer. Utor took a step back and was about to turn around when the door suddenly opened. Now faced with the plight of actually having to speak, Utor stood there looking at the tall figure standing on the threshold. Aware of the obvious fear in the eyes of the child standing before him, the butler smiled and asked, "May I help you young man?"

Utor stammered as he said, "Is M-M-Mr. Lucky here?"

The butler invited Utor into the study to sit and wait.

"May I tell Mr. Lucky who is calling, sir?" said the butler.

"My name is Utor Retting," said Utor.

While Utor waited, a maid brought him

some sweets and a drink. She smiled as she said, "These are for you. I hope you enjoy them."

Utor remained sitting there for what seemed to be an eternity. It was actually only about ten minutes, enough time for him to finish his treat.

When Utor had finished, the butler returned and said, "Mr. Lucky requests that you return again on the morrow at precisely 10 A.M."

Utor thanked the butler and went on his way. He sped away on his bike, and, with each push of the pedals, Utor became more and more relieved. What pressure he faced! He could never have anticipated that much stress. Utor resolved he would never make that journey again.

That night as Utor lay sleeping, he dreamed a beautiful stallion with golden wings swept him up and flew him around Lucky Mountain. It was quite beautiful and bigger than he had ever imagined. Mr. Lucky's land seemed to go on forever.

When Utor awoke he felt this dream must be a sign. He expected Mr. Lucky would be awaiting his return, and thought that telling him about the vision may be his ticket to riches and a life of luxury. Utor could hardly wait to return to Mr. Lucky's mansion.

That morning, Utor, in new spirits, raced up the mountain and knocked on the door. As the butler opened the door, Utor was once again invited into the study where he was given a treat and asked to wait. Again, ten minutes had passed when the butler returned and asked Utor to come again tomorrow at 10 A.M. to see Mr. Lucky.

Utor was dumbfounded. "Why was the vision given to me if nothing were to come of it? Why would Mr. Lucky ask me to come back again tomorrow but not see me, even to intro-duce himself? Am I wasting my time?"

The boy left slowly, his mind full of questions and confusion. He once again thought he should give up his desire to be a writer, since he didn't seem to possess the understanding necessary for such a position.

Utor went to class, where the editor asked him, in front of the class, how his assignment was coming. All eyes peered at him as Utor announced he hadn't met Mr. Lucky yet. The class began laughing at him and telling him he was a failure.

"You will never be a writer, Utor the Bore," was the phrase so prominently ringing in his ears. As the laughing continued, Utor vowed he had to succeed.

The next day, Utor decided he would once again try to see Mr. Lucky. However, the boy again met with the same treatment and instruc tion to return the next day.

This continued for two weeks.

Utor couldn't understand why he continued

to return, especially under the pressure of his classmates making fun of him and calling him a failure. "I am not going to fail! There has got to be a way for me to interview Mr. Lucky. How do I get past his butler? How can I get Mr. Lucky to want to see me?" Utor said to himself.

That night as he slept, he once again dreamed that the beautiful stallion with golden wings swooped him up and carried him around Lucky Mountain. However, this time he noticed that on the back of the Lucky mansion there was a rickety old house that appeared to be attached to the mansion. For some reason this sighting was so poignant and disturbing that it woke him out of his sleep. Utor lay there wondering what the old shack could possibly mean.

As part of what had become Utor's daily routine, he again knocked on the door of the mansion. However, when the butler invited him into the study Utor stopped him saying, "Wait a minute. When you announce my arrival to Mr. Lucky, would you please tell him I am here to talk about the old run-down house attached to the back of the mansion, which I saw in my dream last night as I rode on the back of a beautiful stallion with golden wings." The butler stood there aghast, looking at the young boy. "Very well, sir," he said.

Utor sat in the study waiting but this time no treats were served. He began to wonder what this would mean. The butler returned and escorted him to Mr. Lucky's private office. As the door opened he noticed a man of curious demeanor sitting behind an awe-inspiring work of art, which could hardly be called a desk.

Mr. Lucky invited Utor to sit across from him. As he sat there Mr. Lucky said, "You must be the one."

Utor nervously responded, "What do you mean by 'the one'?"

"I have been meditating for some time, trying to call a special person to me. This person would be able to one day share my secret of success with the world. In my error, I had sought after a man of experience and wisdom. I had not considered that Divinity would send a boy to do such an important work," said Mr. Lucky.

This statement caused Utor to tremble with fear. He then told Mr. Lucky in a timid voice, "I'm only here to write an article for my school newspaper. I have never even written an article yet, and I am a boy of no consequence to men or children. I am not the person you are looking for, Mr. Lucky."

"On the contrary, Mr. Retting. You will write and what you will write will be more than the simple verses of entertainment sought after by your school editor. You will write a book that will be the delight of sages and enlightened men everywhere. You will be the means of calling the wealthy to gather and the passerby to stop and stare. Sit up straight, young man, and strengthen your back, for you are about to take a journey, a journey that will put you on your stallion of golden wings. Come tomorrow at 10 A.M. and you will begin your journey," said Mr. Lucky.

That afternoon as Utor entered his class, the editor once again brazenly remarked, "So, Utor, how are you doing on your assignment thus far?"

Amidst chuckles in the room Utor stated, "I have met with Mr. Lucky, and he is about to teach me how he gained his fortune." Instant silence filled the room. The astonishment was so thick you could cut it with a knife.

CHAPTER 2

Beginning the Journey

*"Our business in life is not to get ahead of others
but to get ahead of ourselves; to break our own records;
to outstrip our yesterdays by our todays; to bear our
trials more beautifully than we ever dreamed we could;
to give as we never have given; to do our work with more
force and a finer finish than ever. This is the true idea:
to get ahead of ourselves."*

CARL HOLMES

Utor arrived promptly as he had for the past two weeks. However, this time he was met at the door by Mr. Lucky himself. Instead of inviting him in, Mr. Lucky directed him to the old shack at the back of the mansion.

As they walked, Mr. Lucky asked Utor to tell him a little about himself. Utor began telling him about his family, friends, and a few other personal details until they came to the back of the mansion. As they stood in front of the old shack, gazing at its lowly existence, Mr. Lucky said, "I suppose this dilapidated old house is not unlike that in which you are living today. I would also guess that your surroundings are as humble as these that have been gathering dust over the years. Am I correct?"

Utor responded, "Similar."

Mr. Lucky continued, "I have kept these old surroundings and this old shack as a reminder of where I came from and who I was. These surroundings are not all that harsh, as I lived quite comfortably here when this was my humble abode. I felt as content and happy as one could be in such circumstances. However, I realized this was the first problem that needed to be solved in my life. This was no way for an honorable, hard-working man to live in a day when opportunity is given to many."

Utor interrupted. "I'm surprised that you could've ever lived in such a place. I assumed your fortune could have only been created over hundreds of years with family money."

"It's true that most people of comparable wealth have generated it over many years, but it is also true that I have amassed such wealth in relatively few years," Mr. Lucky replied.

"Is there a secret to your making so much in so little time?" asked Utor.

"Many people claim they have secrets to gaining wealth. I, on the other hand, know there are simple formulas that can be utilized in creating money, and that it is possible for all to attain great wealth," said Mr. Lucky.

"How is it possible for everyone to attain great wealth when there is only so much wealth to be had in the world?" asked Utor.

"That's where you are wrong, Utor," said Mr. Lucky. "Money is only an idea and there is no end to the available wealth in the world. However, great wealth is created by changing your beliefs."

Utor then said, "I don't understand. How can your beliefs make money?"

"The beliefs to which I refer are the beliefs you have about you. Tell me how you see yourself," said Mr. Lucky.

Utor found it hard to express what he believed about himself, but after a little coaxing, he came up with a few things he realized were holding him back. Utor believed he was shy, clumsy, not very important, scared of people, and not a very good thinker.

Mr. Lucky began to help Utor understand how powerful he really was and shared some of the things that impressed him so far. "Utor, you have already taken steps that will one day lead you to success. You had a problem. This was the same problem that existed with the rest of your colleagues. You all tried to meet with me and I would put you off. This was a test to see how long you would endure. The most any of the rest lasted was five days before quitting. I was not going to talk to anyone who didn't come for at least ten days."

Utor interjected, "I was told this was an easy assignment that anyone could do, but you say that there have been others and none of them had ever even met you?"

"That's right," said Mr. Lucky.

"Well, I had been coming for thirteen days before you ever visited with me. Why did you take so long?" asked Utor.

"I have been waiting for someone who, in my opinion, was not going to take no for an answer," Mr. Lucky responded. "This person had to be someone I could really mentor. However, you will see that the power used in finding opportunities is what I used to find you. The answer to your problem was also the answer to my problem. We both had problems that could only be solved by the uniting of our minds and talents. Since it was unlikely we would ever meet, I'm certain it was Divinity that created the dream that would cause me to believe in you, and you to believe in chance. I have told you enough for one day. Think about what I have said and come back tomorrow with a question for me."

"What kind of question?" asked Utor.

"It doesn't matter, Utor. What matters is that you have a question regarding a problem you desire the answer to," said Mr. Lucky.

CHAPTER 3

What Are Problems?

The Ways

To every man there openeth
A Way, and Ways and a Way.
And the High Soul climbs the High Way,
And the Low Soul gropes the Low,
And in between, on the misty flats,
The rest drift to and fro.
But to every man there openeth
A High Way, and a Low,
And every man decideth
The way his soul shall go.

John Oxenham

T he next day Utor, feeling a little unsure of himself, asked a simple question.

"Mr. Lucky, is your name really I. M. Lucky? People say you must be egotistical and pretentious to take a name like I. M. Lucky."

"Why do you ask such a question, Utor?"

"Well, it was one of the questions on my assignment," answered Utor.

"But is it a question you want the answer to?" queried Mr. Lucky.

Utor sat there with his thoughts for a moment. Then, as though a burst of energy had hit him, he blurted out, "Yes! I want to know why you use that name because it does sound rather vain, and if you are going to be my mentor, then I should know what kind of guy I am dealing with."

Mr. Lucky smiled and said, "You have a problem, Utor."

"What problem?" asked Utor.

"Before you can solve a problem, you must first realize that you have a problem. So I will ask you, Utor, what is your problem?"

Utor sat there baffled and confused. He thought to himself, "All I want to know is his name. How does that make me have a problem?" Then it hit him. "I get it. My problem is not what your name is, but what my feelings about your name are doing to me," he said.

"That is correct," said Mr. Lucky. "Utor, you have a problem in being able to accept the full training I can give you, because before you ever met me you believed something negative about me. You have limited your capacity to learn from me because of an unfounded belief, which is your problem. I am going to share with you the secret of my success that I want you to share with the world. The secret is in our understanding of and the way we deal with problems.

"Please pay attention, Utor," said Mr. Lucky. "The problem with most problems is our belief that the problem is a problem. Problems are *opportunities,* and the person filled with the wisdom of this perspective is the person who will one day be considered a genius, a hero, or any number of a thousand accolades. The world and its host of inventions, ideas, and marvelous creations are a tribute to man's ability to turn problems into opportunities.

"Unresolved problems are nothing more than one's inability to focus on the probable positive outcome that could result from focusing one's attention on a solution. In other words, it is the inability to realize the opportunity the problem presents. However, if you utilize your creativity and ingenuity, you would realize the opportunity your problem proffers you. To one, problems are exciting. Problems have the ability to direct your mind to that glorious state of introspection where you are able to receive inspiration, genius, and personal value. To another, problems are fearful, impenetrable walls of failure, deficiency, and self-defeat. Your beliefs and desires determine the way you experience it. If you believe in solutions and desire opportunity, then answers will inevitably flow from that special realm where talent and brilliance originate.

"If you believe in problems and desire to avoid the exertion involved in solving problems, then you are doomed to the hell of complacency, weakness, and struggle.

"When a problem is viewed as an opportunity, the solution to that problem will somehow materialize in a number of positive manifestations. However, when your belief is that the problem is a 'problem,' the only relative solution is to find fault with the problem and engulf your mind in the miseries and woes to which unresolved problems inevitably evolve. Therefore, it is in our best interest to view a problem not only as something in need of a solution, but a solution to something that can somehow be reinvented into an opportunity."

Utor was quite puzzled by Mr. Lucky's remarks. He sat there trying to ingest it all, but there was too much for him to handle. Mr. Lucky could see that Utor was at a point where reflection was more important than new information. He told Utor it would be best for him to go home and think about what he had learned so far, and to come again the next day for further instructions.

Utor was heading for the door when he realized that his question had not been answered. He turned back to Mr. Lucky and said, "Wait a minute, Mr. Lucky! You never did tell me about your name."

Mr. Lucky smiled, nodded, and began walking toward Utor as he said, "You are right, Utor, I wasn't going to tell you yet, but since you have remembered to focus on your problem I will answer you.

"My name must always remain a secret until I die, unless you find others, such as your-self, who can understand its meaning and what it does for the general public. It is really quite simple when you think about it. My name is Ivan McIntyre, hence the I. M. The Lucky part is the name I adopted because it was what most people in the community used for me. How many times have you heard people in town, referring to me, say, 'he sure is lucky'? Of course, everyone does. In fact, they said it so often that I changed my name to make it easier for them to hold to their illusion."

"What illusion?" asked Utor.

"The illusion that my success is due to luck. So long as they can believe this, they don't have to put forth any effort to be successful themselves. They have no idea that my success is due to my ability to turn problems into opportunities. Successes, such as you see before you, could never come from one man's luck. This level of success comes only through the power of multiple minds working together in a combined effort to turn problems into opportunities," said Mr. Lucky.

"So you mean that I. M. Lucky is not meant to have the undertone the people in town have given it?" asked Utor.

Mr. Lucky simply smiled as he turned to go upstairs.

CHAPTER 4

Looking Beyond
the Solution

"Don't bring me your successes, for they weaken me; rather, bring me your problems, for they strengthen me."

Boss Kettering, former president, General Motors

Once again, Utor arrived at the usual time. As he and Mr. Lucky sat down for another discussion, Mr. Lucky asked, "So, Utor, have you got any questions for me today?"

Utor responded by telling Mr. Lucky, "I spent most of the day thinking about what you told me, the part about a person's view of problems, and I realized that I have done the same thing. I have a problem getting along with my peers, and I believed I solved my problem by walking away from them. However, when I thought about what you said yesterday, the part about turning problems into opportunities, I couldn't see how my walking away could give me an opportunity. I understand solving problems, but what do you mean when you say, 'Turn the problem into an opportunity'?"

Mr. Lucky paused for a moment because he was amazed at Utor's ability to conceptualize what he had been taught so far. He then said to Utor, "That is a very astute question, Utor. You have obviously been giving this serious thought. I can now see why you were sent to me."

Leaning toward him, Mr. Lucky looked deep into Utor's eyes and said, "When you see a problem what do you see? Most people see suffering, work, scarcity, disillusionment, and a thousand other negative affects. I see opportunity. Let me give you a simple example. Let's say you have a problem. You have only one ear of corn and you are hungry. What would be your solution?"

"Eat the ear of corn," said Utor.

"As it would be for the thousands of people in the village below," said Mr. Lucky. "Now,

Utor, tell me what opportunity you could see in this problem."

Utor thought for a while then looked down and said, "I'm sorry, Mr. Lucky, but I am too ignorant to find an opportunity for the problem."

"Nonsense, Utor," said Mr. Lucky. "You have been trained to find defeat rather than opportunity and immediate gratification rather than the fruits of patience. With a little practice, you, too, will be able to find the opportunity in any problem.

"You were successful in finding a solution but the opportunity seemed much more elusive, when in actuality it was very simple. If you eat the ear of corn, you will be hungry in a few hours and find yourself foraging for food again. The opportunity is to save the ear of corn and search for other food. If you sacrifice the desire to eat corn now, it will yield hundreds or even thousands of ears if you plant the kernels and wait a season to eat. Not only will you have enough corn to feed you for the rest of the year, but you will have more ears to plant a crop double the size for the next season."

Utor's eyes lit up, and Mr. Lucky noticed that hidden attribute in Utor, which each person finds when first realizing opportunity.

"I perceive that your mind has been opened to opportunity, Utor, so I will give you another example," said Mr. Lucky.

Mr. Lucky gave Utor the following problem: "You know the best process for assembling widgets, but your employee thinks he has a better way. Even though all logic, engineering information, and common sense says your way is better, he still wants to try his way. What is the obvious solution you think most people would find?"

Utor responded, "They would probably tell the employee to do it the employer's way or be fired."

"Unfortunately, you are probably correct, Utor. But what opportunity could you find in such a problem?" asked Mr. Lucky.

Utor paused for a minute, deep in thought as he peered into Mr. Lucky's eyes. Instead of looking down and considering himself igno-rant, Utor smiled as he looked at Mr. Lucky and said, "I don't know, but I can't wait to find out."

Mr. Lucky smiled and said, "Very good, Utor, you have overcome the temptation to believe in defeat and you are now looking for opportunity. Here is another lesson in looking for opportunity: You don't have to be the one with the answer. It is good that you are expect-ing an answer from someone else."

Mr. Lucky continued, "The opportunity would be to tell the employee, 'All the facts I have in hand prove my way is best, and I believe that if you follow my direction you will be able to assemble 100 widgets a week. However, I'll give you a chance to prove yourself. If you can assemble more than 100 widgets each week on a regular basis, I will let you continue your process and give you a raise for your dedication and innovation.'

"Now you may ask, how is this to be considered an opportunity? If you force the employee to do it your way he will do it reluctantly and probably never even reach 100 widgets a week because he would subconsciously or consciously hope your plan would fail. When you challenge him with a promise to reward his excellence then he will do everything in his power to prove his way is best and he will assemble 120 or 150 or even 200 widgets just to prove his way will work. Not only will your company assemble up to twice the amount of widgets and make the profits from such a feat, but you will also have a very loyal employee who will look for additional opportunities to prove his worth to you. This is where innovation can come to your company and build wealth beyond your belief."

Utor was astounded at the clarity this brought to his mind. He looked at Mr. Lucky and said, "That is amazing! Give me another example to see if I can find the opportunity."

Mr. Lucky thought for a moment and then said, "Your car breaks down and you have no money to buy a new one. What is your solution?"

Utor was quick to respond, almost sarcastically, because he knew this was not the end result, "Get a loan at 12 percent interest and pay double for a car in the end."

"That is correct, Utor," said Mr. Lucky. "Now tell me the opportunity."

Utor again smiled and said, "I don't know. What is it?"

Mr. Lucky replied, "No, Utor, not this time.

You need to start practicing yourself or you will never open that creative part of your mind, which is in a steady slumber in the heads of most people. I will help prepare lunch while you sit there and find an opportunity to the problem."

Mr. Lucky walked out of the room and Utor became a little nervous as he sat there thinking. Coming up with an opportunity seemed like an arduous task for one so young as Utor, but with the new confidence that opportunities really exist, he became determined to come up with one.

When Mr. Lucky re-entered the room with a delightful salad and scones, Utor was filled with uncontainable excitement.

"I got it, Mr. Lucky! I got it! I would find five companies that would pay me $1,000 a month each to paint their logo and phone number on the beautiful $85,000 Lamborghini

Diablo that I would purchase. I would get a loan at 8 percent interest for two years, which will have a monthly payment of about $3,850. I would save the extra $1,150 per month to put toward the new paint job at the end of the two years. In two years, I will own a beautiful $85,000 car with a brand-new paint job. I could then sell the car for $75,000 and buy a more modest vehicle for $30,000. I would put the other $45,000 toward a down payment on my new house."

"Very good, Utor. Your idea was even better than mine. You see, you can find opportunities amidst problems. You are on your way to a life of success, Utor, but there is more for me to teach you. Come back tomorrow and we will continue our discussion," said Mr. Lucky.

Later that day, Utor entered his writing class jumping up and down saying, "I am going to be rich beyond my wildest dreams."

The class went silent.

"Mr. Lucky has shared with me the secret of success and now there is nothing that can stop me!"

The school editor then said, in his snide manner, "Oh, yeah? Well, what about the 'F' you will receive in this class and in Mr. Grind's? You have been spending so much time with Mr. Lucky that you haven't been accomplishing the assigned tasks, so you are bound to fail."

Utor's eyes filled with excitement as he got up and said, "What a great opportunity! You don't realize this, but if you fail me you will give me a chance to become even more powerful than I could be if you passed me."

The class was terribly surprised, and the editor was dumbfounded, as Utor happily walked out of the class buoyant and self-assured. When Utor returned home he found his mother and father waiting for him at the door.

"We just received a call from the editor of your school newspaper and he told us what you have been doing. Son, you had better pass your classes or you will never amount to anything throughout your life," said his father.

Utor responded, "Dad, Mom, you will never believe what has happened to me. Mr. Lucky has opened my mind and taught me how to succeed in the midst of failure. There is nothing the editor, school, or my classmates could ever do to keep me from succeeding in life. I am learning how to overcome any problem or obstacle in life, and I can see that one day I will be like Mr. Lucky, and you will, too. I have learned that when a problem arises, with a little intelligent thinking you can find a solution. With a little intelligent thinking, coupled with creative imagination, you can find an opportunity. I only hope you will support me through this new adventure."

Utor's father and mother were astounded at the change that had come over their lumbering, shy boy. Never had they seen him so happy and excited. Although in the future they received more calls from the school, they decided to support their son.

CHAPTER 5

What's Holding You Back?

*"We cannot all be John Cabots, sailing off into
the blue with the king's patent to discover new lands;
but we can be explorers in spirit, with democracy's
mandate to make this land better by discovering
new ways of living and doing things.*

*The spirit of exploration, whether it be of the
surface of the earth or the principles of living greatly,
includes developing the capacity to face trouble
with courage, disappointment with cheerfulness,
and triumph with humility."*

ROYAL BANK OF CANADA NEWSLETTER

U tor raced to Mr. Lucky's mansion only to find him gone. He asked the butler where he could find him but the butler was uncertain. "He said only that he will be in town observing business," explained the butler.

Utor turned sadly and began the path for home. While on his way he thought to himself, "I have a problem. The problem is that I expected further training from Mr. Lucky today, but he is not there. The solution is to go home or to school. But, what is the opportunity?" As he continued down the path it came to him. "What better opportunity than to be with Mr. Lucky as he observes business. I will find him and observe with him."

Utor went from business to business

seeking the whereabouts of Mr. Lucky. Although he had no idea where to begin, he knew somehow he would be guided to Mr. Lucky, if that was really in his best interest. In less than thirty minutes, Utor found Mr. Lucky. Utor said, as he approached him, "Why didn't you tell me you were coming to town? I would have met you here."

"I was testing you, Utor," Mr. Lucky replied. "I knew if this were important enough to you that you would find me. Time for your next lesson."

As they walked down the street Mr. Lucky said, "The nature of man is generally lazy. Rather than work a solution to a problem he prefers to solve the problem of work. One of the first abilities the human mind will master is the art of finding a good excuse. It is much easier for a person to say, 'I can't do it' than it is to just do it. Casting blame is the next beloved attribute so important in limiting one's ability to solve problems. However, when it comes to finding opportunities, which go beyond solutions, the hindrance we experience can generally be attributed to our beliefs. The primary beliefs that keep us from solving our problems are what you will see in the attitudes of the people in the floundering businesses of this town."

The first business they entered was Jim's Jewelers.

"Hi, Jim," said Mr. Lucky.

"Hello, Mr. Lucky," said Jim with the sound of discouragement in his voice.

"What seems to be the problem?" said Mr. Lucky.

"I have been audited by the IRS and they say I owe them another $3,000. I have been going through my receipts, and I don't know how they can figure I owe this amount," responded Jim.

Mr. Lucky quickly replied, "Why don't you

call Kate, the tax accountant? Maybe she can help you."

In a tired voice Jim replied, "I don't know her well, and I don't know if I could trust her. Besides, I can't afford to pay out more money with this bill hanging over my head."

Mr. Lucky said in a somewhat somber tone, "It sounds like you can't afford not to use her. Good luck to you, Jim."

With that they left the building.

As they walked down the street Mr. Lucky turned to Utor and said, "That is one of the classic reasons people can't solve their problems. Can you figure it out?"

Utor thought for a moment then said, "He should have listened to you."

Mr. Lucky replied, "Well, Utor, you are partly right. Take out your notepad and pen and write this down. At the top write, *Why People Can't Solve Problems.* Underneath that write:

1. YOU BELIEVE YOU HAVE TO SOLVE YOUR OWN PROBLEM.

"With this reason in mind, can you figure out a solution to Jim's problem?"

"I think so," said Utor. "If Jim would solicit the help of Kate, the tax accountant, she could solve his problem, but he thinks he has to solve it himself so he is left in a lurch trying to do something he is not so talented at."

"That is correct," said Mr. Lucky. "You have solved his problem, now tell me what could be the opportunity for Jim."

Utor paused for a moment then said, "If he used Kate's services, he could potentially save hundreds or thousands of dollars, plus he would be able to spend more of his time on his business, or with his family, instead of making himself miserable trying to do something that he is obviously not very good at."

Mr. Lucky said, "Very good, Utor. You are picking up on this much faster than I would have given you credit for."

They entered the next store—Tanner's Nickel & Dime. As they entered, they found Mr. Tanner talking to the police. They patiently waited until the police had finished their business and left.

"What's the problem, Mr. Tanner?" asked Mr. Lucky.

In an angry voice Mr. Tanner said, "Those rotten hoodlums! Always stealing from me. Do they think I am so rich that it doesn't cause my family to suffer? I lose almost 10 percent of my profits each year to shoplifters, and if this doesn't stop, I may end up going out of business."

"What do you plan on doing about it?" asked Mr. Lucky.

You could hear the defeat in Mr. Tanner's voice as he said, "What can I do? Security systems, bars on the doors; it all costs money and that is what I don't have."

"Sorry to hear of your misfortune, Mr. Tanner. Good luck to you until we meet again," said Mr. Lucky.

As they left, Mr. Lucky again turned to Utor and asked, "What was his problem?"

"Was it that he was depressed?" asked Utor.

Mr. Lucky pointed to Utor's pocket and said, "Take out your notepad and write:

2. YOU BELIEVE YOU CAN'T SOLVE YOUR PROBLEM.

"Because Mr. Tanner did not believe he could solve his problem, the only solution he had in his mind was to close his business, which is probably what will happen."

Utor was perplexed and said, "I know what his problem is, but what is the solution if he can't afford a security system?" Mr. Lucky responded, "You err in what you assume the problem is. His problem is not the theft, nor is it the lack of money to buy a security system. His problem is what you wrote down in your notepad under number two. However, let us assume that number two is not his problem, and we will solve the problems of his security and lack of money. Have you noticed the attitude of Mr. Tanner?"

Utor replied, "Why yes, I have. He is a crotchety old man, ill willed, and rather mean."

Mr. Lucky continued, "And did you notice the large sign he has hanging on the front entrance?"

Utor replied, "Yeah, it said, 'You break it you buy it.'"

Mr. Lucky began to teach Utor a little about human psychology when he said, "People generally don't want to hurt kind-hearted people. A person as mean, selfish, and uncaring as Mr. Tanner is an easy target for the mischievous. Ten percent of his profits is a high number compared to the other stores in town, who experience a more tolerable amount of only 2 percent theft. The solution to Mr. Tanner's problem is for him to tear down that sign and begin being nice to people. The opportunity lies on a more emotional and spiritual level for him, and it will also help him financially.

If Mr. Tanner would be nicer, he would have more business, less thievery, a happier countenance, and many more friends. In short, life would become a sweet joy to him."

The next business they entered was the tax accountant's.

"Hello, Kate, how are you this fine day?" said Mr. Lucky.

Kate responded, "Oh, just fine, Mr. Lucky. It's always a pleasure to see you. By the way, thank you for that advice you gave me a few months ago. My business has been thriving ever since."

"Kate," said Mr. Lucky, "Your business is thriving, and you seem cheerful, but I believe you are putting on a façade. Is something the matter?"

Kate paused and looked down. When she lifted her head she said, "I have been working so hard, finally making enough money so that my husband and I could buy a bigger house and a new car. I thought this would take the pressures off our marriage so we could be happy and spend more quality time together. Now I am working so much that we hardly have any time for each other. I am worried that our marriage may not make it." Kate was welling up with emotion when Mr. Lucky walked forward to give her a hug.

Mr. Lucky then said, "Kate, the advice I gave you months ago was to help you with your struggling business and it worked. Will you now hear my advice to help your struggling marriage?"

Kate was too full of emotion to speak so she just nodded.

Mr. Lucky continued, "You gave more time to your business to make it work, why don't you try giving more time to your marriage to make it work? I know you work many evenings in here and your husband works days. By the time you get home from a hard day of thinking and running numbers you are probably too exhausted to spend any quality or intimate time with your husband. As a man, he would probably interpret this as a rejection of him personally, and he is now rejecting you because of it. I know it is hard to spend the time to run your business the way you have and still have time at home, but maybe it is time to hire someone to take over the increased business you have experienced so you can spend more time at home. You may have to sell the car, but it's better than selling the marriage."

Kate looked up and with tears in her eyes she smiled and said, "Thank you, Mr. Lucky. That is what I wanted to do, but I was too afraid of losing the income. I guess I just needed to hear, from someone else, that it was the right thing to do."

They exchanged a few more words, and then Utor and Mr. Lucky were on their way. As they left, Mr. Lucky asked Utor, "Do you know what the problem was in there?"

Utor responded, "I was so nervous and scared for her that I stopped thinking of problems and solutions."

"I understand, Utor," said Mr. Lucky. "It is often quite difficult to think clearly when you are in an emotional state. Good decisions are seldom made when you are overemotional. When you are the one helping, it is your responsibility to not become too emotionally attached, even though it may seem like the best thing to do at the time.

"Take out your notepad and write:

3. YOU MISINTERPRET WHAT THE PROBLEM REALLY IS.

"Kate's real problem was that she and her husband were not happy in their marriage. Kate thought her problem was not enough money so she increased her business to make more money. However, the additional time away from the family increased her real problem. The opportunity here is another one that brings joy rather than money. If Kate and her husband decide together to make the sacrifice of money for more family time, they will feel a renewed passion for their children and their time together, which will bring them greater rewards than the additional money ever could."

Utor was quiet now as they walked down the street. Mr. Lucky perceived that Utor needed some time to sort out his thoughts, so he skipped a few businesses and continued walking for a time in silence.

Suddenly, Utor received an epiphany and excitedly exclaimed, "Wait a minute! I get it.

Opportunities are not always based on material wealth. So then, an opportunity is anything that personally benefits you. Is that right?"

"Almost," said Mr. Lucky. "An opportunity is anything that benefits you as well as others. Always remember that your success will grow faster when you can combine your success with that of your friends, family, and business associates. Don't ever lose sight of the revelation you have just received and realize that although we are concentrating on how to find financial opportunities, there are always spiritual, physical, social, and emotional opportunities that lie before you as well."

As Mr. Lucky finished speaking, they walked into a foundry. Mr. Lucky asked the receptionist if she would tell Mr. Cambridge that he was there. In a moment, they were ushered into a plush office filled with awards and certificates hanging on the wall. Mr.

Cambridge seemed happy to see Mr. Lucky.

After exchanging salutations, Mr. Cambridge looked over at Utor and said, "So whom do we have here?"

Mr. Lucky introduced Utor and explained why he was with him. He then asked Mr. Cambridge if he had any advice for Utor.

Mr. Cambridge looked sternly at Utor, which made Utor very nervous. Then Mr. Cambridge changed his stern face into a big smile and said, "Do you realize the opportunity that has been given to you, young man?"

Utor didn't say a thing but simply shrugged his shoulders.

Mr. Cambridge continued, "You happen to be in the company of two of the wealthiest and wisest men in the country. Thousands of people would give up their children to be in your place right now, and many would give up their children for much less." They all laughed, as it was obvious

Mr. Cambridge was using humor to help take the pressure of the meeting off Utor.

Mr. Cambridge said, "Son, I have a little story to share with you. There was once a man who was struggling to get a business off the ground. He had a vision that included hundreds of people selling thousands of tools all over the country. Although he was quite a bright and cunning fellow, he had a few problems. He was selling tools to the masses, but his service began to suffer under the mound of paperwork caused by so many small orders and the time and expense caused by all the various packaging methods required to send each item. Customers were complaining that it was taking too long to fill their orders, and they were beginning to go to the competition.

"His solution was to hire more people to package, ship, and manage the accounting. However, the overhead was getting so high that he was about to raise his prices to a level that would price him out of the market. Luckily, this bright fellow decided to seek the counsel of a successful friend who gave him the advice that turned his operation into the most successful business in his industry. The advice was to stop trying to deal with each individual customer. He actually advised that he get rid of his customers. Now, I ask you, does that sound like very sound advice?"

Utor cautiously said, "No."

Then Mr. Cambridge said, "Well, that is just what the old fool did. He immediately started hiring distributors to deal with the individuals, while he only dealt with the distributors. Sure, he had to give up some of the profits to the distributors, but he went from having many thousands of customers to dealing with only a few hundred. He required a minimum purchase amount each time they bought, and this changed his packaging into only three different box sizes. He was able to turn some of his packaging and shipping crew into salespeople, who were very successful at finding distributors. He became one of the richest men in the country by turning out a quality product with great efficiency and at a decent price. Now, Utor, I will tell you who the men in this story were; the bright old fool was myself and the advisor was Mr. Lucky. And this was before he, too, created his mountain of wealth.

"Over the years, Mr. Lucky and I developed a problem-solving method that far surpassed the abilities of the common man. It is because of this technique that we have achieved the level of success you see today. The trick is to not look for *solutions* to problems but for *opportunities.* I am sorry for cutting this short but I have some pressing business to attend to. Young man, if you have acquired the camaraderie of Mr.

Lucky, my only advice to you is to listen to this man, for he can do nothing but guide you to success. Good day, my friends."

Mr. Cambridge happily walked out to his foundry while Utor and Mr. Lucky headed for the exit. On the way out Mr. Lucky asked Utor, "Do you understand what his original problem was?" Utor said, "He thought he knew how to make his business successful but it didn't work. He needed your help."

"Very close, Utor," said Mr. Lucky. He then told Utor to get out his notebook and write:

4. YOU BELIEVE THE SOLUTION MUST MATERIALIZE THE WAY YOU WANT IT TO.

"He had a plan and he was trying to force his plan to work," said Mr. Lucky. "However, logistics would prove it was impossible for his plan to succeed. I knew the solution to his problem was to get the details out of his hands. It was my search for an opportunity that gave me the idea to hire distributors who would deal with the individuals, plus share in the cost of advertising, which would cause them to sell even more."

As they continued walking down the street, they happened to come upon a beggar. As he asked for money, Mr. Lucky stopped and said, "Why do you need money, sir?"

The beggar said, "Because I have none, Mr. Lucky, and you have it all."

Utor was surprised as Mr. Lucky proceeded to sit next to the beggar and converse with him. Mr. Lucky asked the beggar to please tell his story.

The beggar began, "I had a wife, four kids, and a leather shop that was very successful in my father's day, but now the price of leather is too high and nobody can afford it anymore. I lost my business, nobody would hire me, and my wife left me."

Mr. Lucky then said, "I am wearing a pair of

$700 leather boots and a $75 leather belt. It wasn't the price of leather that killed your business, but the change of customer that you missed. You were still selling to the general populace when you should have been targeting the wealthy and charging extra for your services. However, even if you would have gone after the right market you still would have failed."

"And just why is that?" asked the beggar indignantly.

Mr. Lucky retorted, "Because you blame the customer, prices, your family, and your father for your problems. You never looked for the solution. Had you searched for solutions, you would probably have found an opportunity to sell to others, like me, your $100 pair of boots for $700. If you will stop blaming others for your problems and quit putting your hand out for someone else's leftovers, you just might find a way back into life and society."

With that Mr. Lucky got up and proceeded to leave when the beggar hollered out, "Hey, aren't you going to give me anything?"

Mr. Lucky walked back to the beggar, squatted down before him to eye level, and said, "Mister, every person who puts a penny in that hand of yours is robbing you of opportunity. I have given you thousands of dollars in value if you will but get up and get it." He then turned and walked away.

As they walked, Utor pulled out his notepad and said, "There was a very obvious lesson there and I am ready to write it down."

Mr. Lucky simply said:

5. YOU BELIEVE THAT SOMETHING OUT OF YOUR CONTROL IS STOPPING YOU FROM FINDING A SOLUTION.

"You see, Utor, some people think they don't have a job because no one will hire them. The problem is that they are in their living room watching TV and sitting next to a phone. They

figure they are doing their part by waiting for
the phone to ring. If it doesn't ring with someone begging them to work for them, then it is
the phone's fault."

Next they entered Mrs. Larcy's shop. Mrs.
Larcy was in the back working on a painting and
didn't hear them come in. Mr. Lucky chose not
to disturb her, so they just looked around. In
whispered tones Mr. Lucky said to Utor,
"Excellent work, isn't it? Mrs. Larcy is a most
exquisite artist but of no renown. She has sold
only a few pieces of her stupendous work,
because she feels they are never good enough.
From one week to the next she improves on
perfection. However, once she discovers a new
technique she feels she can no longer sell the
piece she created a week ago because it is not of
the higher quality. Nothing but the best must
leave her shop. Because of her problem, her
business remains a hobby instead of a business.

Do you know what her problem is, Utor?"

Utor thought about it, but couldn't figure it out because he thought that expecting the highest quality from your company would be a good way of keeping a long-term business. Utor finally replied, "No, I don't see her problem."

Mr. Lucky told Utor to get out his notepad and write:

6. YOU ARE TRYING TO SOLVE A PROBLEM THAT IS NOT REALLY A PROBLEM.

"Utor," said Mr. Lucky, "every day in business you should be looking for ways to improve your quality, service, and price, but you must also realize that there comes a time when a product is good enough for your customers. Yesterday, Mrs. Larcy created a piece she was proud of, and which many people would love to have hanging in their living room today. However, today Mrs. Larcy sees a way it could be improved, so she continues to improve and

improve and the people are left with no picture
to adorn their living room. When you are in the
process of developing, you must decide at what
point your product will have enough benefit to
be of value to the customer, and then sell it. Even
though you know in a month or two you will have
a product far superior to the one you are selling
today, you still sell the beneficial product today.

"So, Utor, what is Mrs. Larcy's problem?"

Utor quickly responded, "She is not selling
many of her works of art that would benefit her
customers and make her enough money to turn
a hobby into a business profession."

"Excellent, Utor. And what would be her
opportunity?" asked Mr. Lucky.

Utor didn't have to think long, as his mind
was beginning to think *opportunity* instead of
just *solution*. "She could hire an art distributor
to make reprints and sell them worldwide.
She could have her own art studio to sell her

originals, and go on tour around the world offering speaking engagements and being paid thousands as an art consultant."

Mr. Lucky laughed as he said, "Utor, I think I may have created a monster. Your mind has really turned on to seeking opportunity, and you are doing very well. It is good to dream and plan for bigger and better things, but keep your mind on productive opportunities, not opportunities for personal grandeur, as those are usually self-defeating in the end."

They next entered a manufacturing facility where everyone seemed to be unhappy and just doing their jobs. Utor felt a little uncomfortable as he said, "What's wrong here? I have never seen so many miserable people. Are they not paid well?"

Just then, Mr. Lucky turned to a very exuberant individual who loudly exclaimed, "Mr. Lucky, how are you doing?"

"Fine, Ted, and how is business today?" asked Mr. Lucky.

Ted shook his head and said, "I don't know what's wrong with the help these days. It seems I can't get production on-line and it is costing the company thousands of dollars an hour. My head is in a noose because I told headquarters we would be operational two days ago and we are still trying to get the assembly line working properly. I have been riding these people for a month and they are still just lollygagging around."

Mr. Lucky asked Ted, "What made you think you could have it operational two days ago?"

"Experience," said Ted with his chest puffed out.

Mr. Lucky rejoined, "Yours or theirs?"

Ted thought for a minute then said, "Come to think of it, my last crew was much more experienced than this crew, and I have probably expected too much of them."

Mr. Lucky turned to the working floor where several zombielike bodies were mulling around and said, "You know what I see? I see a crew of discouraged individuals who need a leader to step up and accept responsibility for their shortcomings, and apologize for demanding much more than their skill level was capable of accomplishing. I bet you would create a faster step and a clearer mind in those people if you led them in such a way. You would give them a whole new reason to get you operational and they would be happier doing it. When you explain your new understanding to headquarters, they will be more forgiving as well."

Ted excitedly exclaimed, "You're right! I'll do it." Ted started jogging for the stairs to get down to his crew, when he suddenly stopped and turned back to Mr. Lucky and Utor and said, "I'm sorry, in my excitement I forgot my manners. What did you come here for, Mr. Lucky?"

Mr. Lucky smiled and said, "You never mind, it's nothing that can't wait for another visit. Go and fix your problem."

As they left, Mr. Lucky once again asked Utor, "What was his problem?"

Utor responded, "He was expecting more out of his crew then he should have."

"That is correct, Utor, but why did he expect more? It was because of number seven. Take out your notepad, Utor, and write:

7. YOU PUT A TIME LIMIT ON WHEN YOU BELIEVE THE PROBLEM SHOULD BE SOLVED.

"Many people suffer through a mid-life crisis because they put a time limit on when they think they should be successful. Others punish friends and family because a task was not finished when they thought it should be. When you can look at a solution in terms of the opportunity, instead of the time it takes to solve a problem, your desire for the opportunity will far outweigh the patience required to get it done. So now, Utor, we have defined his problem but what was his opportunity?"

Utor responded, "By setting realistic, achievable goals for his crew, he would become productive faster and would develop a more loyal working crew."

"That is exactly what I would have said, Utor," said Mr. Lucky.

Mr. Lucky offered to take Utor to lunch. They sat down, and Mr. Lucky was obviously surprised to find Quinn waiting on them.

"Quinn, what are you doing working here?" asked Mr. Lucky.

Quinn carried a look of hopelessness as he said, "I closed down the business. I tried for three months to get the word out, but the business wasn't making any money, so I stopped before I lost any more money in it."

Mr. Lucky seemed almost angry as he said in hushed tones, "Quinn, you told me you had enough money to sustain your business for one year. I told you it would take six months to realize a profit, and a year to generate enough money to receive the income level you were used to living on. After that, you would start making enough to put toward retirement. Why did you quit so early?"

Quinn simply said, as he shook his head, "There was no money coming in and I got scared. May I take your order, Mr. Lucky?"

Mr. Lucky despondently turned his eyes to the menu and said, "I'll need a minute." Quinn walked away slowly in an attitude of defeat.

Utor, concerned with the heavy moment and not really knowing what to do or say, slowly pulled out his notepad and wrote:

8. YOU BELIEVE YOU MUST GIVE UP PREMATURELY.

He started to slowly put the notepad away

when Mr. Lucky said, with his eyes still in his menu, "What did you write, Utor?" Utor told him, and Mr. Lucky lowered the menu to reveal the smile on his face.

Mr. Lucky then said, "What do you think was going through my head, Utor?"

Utor replied, "I suppose disappointment for the young man's misfortune."

"The young man did not have a misfortune, he had a problem. What was going through my head, Utor?" Mr. Lucky asked with greater intensity.

Utor smiled and said, "You were looking for the opportunity."

Just then, Quinn came back with his sullen face and said, "What can I get you, sir?"

Mr. Lucky sat up, looked at him directly, and said, "Well, first you can get me a smile, then you can get me a waiter. You are no waiter. You are a businessman, and you will quit this job right now and sit here while we talk, and I buy you lunch."

Mr. Lucky proceeded to offer Quinn words of encouragement as well as his direct number for Quinn to contact him whenever he felt scared enough to want to quit. Lunch ended and Mr. Lucky and Utor headed back toward the end of town.

On their way, they ran into Anna. Anna was a young divorcée with no children, who had a rather dark opinion of herself.

"How are you this fine day, Anna?" said Mr. Lucky.

Anna smiled and said, "Oh, fine I guess."

"I guess?" said Mr. Lucky, "And how is that attitude supposed to help you?"

Anna put her head down and said, "I'm sorry, Mr. Lucky, but I am not in the mood for a positive-thinking lecture right now. I was just fired from my job. I can't seem to do anything right. Good day, Mr. Lucky." And with that she left.

Mr. Lucky turned to Utor and asked, "What was the problem there, Utor?"

Utor guessed, "Self defeat?"

Mr. Lucky said, "Close:

9. YOU BELIEVE THE PROBLEM IS YOU.

"Any time you believe you are the problem, a solution is slow to come by. This is because you are generally your own worst critic, and any solution you come up with will not be good enough for you. Anna believes she can't do anything right, and that her problems are all because of her ineptness. Therefore, she only notices her mistakes in life. She never notices how she brings joy into the hearts of people each time she simply flashes her beautiful smile. It is a hard one to recover from, even though you could obviously see the astounding level of opportunities that would come by solving this problem."

After looking at his watch, Mr. Lucky continued, "I'm sorry, Utor, but due to time constraints I must leave, so I will give you the last erroneous belief I want you to learn today. Write:

10. YOU ARE LAZY.

"Although this one doesn't seem like a belief, it actually is. It is the belief that resting is more important than following opportunities. Millions of people give up their dreams and ideals simply because it takes effort to attain them.

There are many other beliefs that keep us from finding solutions and opportunities to problems, but you must discover some of them for yourself, so for today I will limit my comments to the ten beliefs given you thus far."

With that, Mr. Lucky headed back to his mansion.

CHAPTER 6

Resource Masterminding

"You see things and you say, 'Why?'
But I dream things that never were, and I say,
'Why not?'"

GEORGE BERNARD SHAW

The next day Mr. Lucky sat Utor down and said, "Utor, today you need to learn the simple process of problem solving. There have been many elaborate plans, programs, and classes designed to teach various levels of problem solving.

"There are mathematical systems, physics systems, psychological, and many others. But when we go beyond problem solving to finding opportunities, for me there is only one system that works consistently and dependably. It is a system that couples resources with inspiration. I call this system *Resource Masterminding*. It is a simple four-step process anyone can do. The steps are as follows."

Resource Masterminding

1. *Find the real problem.* Break down a problem to what would be considered the real problem.

2. *Discover.* Discover what resources are—or could be—available to work on the problem.

3. *Condense.* Utilize the best resources on your list.

4. *Synergize.* Combine those resources to generate the synergy needed to create a masterful opportunity.

"Before we begin to work on this, I am going to list on the whiteboard the mistaken beliefs we observed yesterday," Mr. Lucky said.

Mr. Lucky wrote the following:

Mistaken Beliefs

1. You believe you have to solve your own problem.

2. You believe you can't solve your problem.

3. You misinterpret what the problem really is.

4. You believe the solution must materialize the way you want it to.

5. You believe that something out of your

control is stopping you from finding a solution.

6. You are trying to solve a problem that is not really a problem.

7. You put a time limit on when you believe the problem should be solved.

8. You believe you must give up prematurely.

9. You believe the problem is you.

10. You are lazy.

Mr. Lucky continued. "Mistaken beliefs keep us from recognizing our real problem. Let's begin by working on a real problem. Give me an example of a problem you are experiencing right now, Utor."

Utor thought for a moment and said, "Nobody likes me. I don't have any friends."

Mr. Lucky rejoined, "Let's take this to step number one. Is this the real problem?"

Utor responded, "It's mighty real to me."

Mr. Lucky chuckled as he said, "Yes, Utor, I'm sure this is a real problem for you, but is it the actual problem or is this only the *result* of the actual problem? Read number three on the Mistaken Beliefs list."

Utor read aloud, "You misinterpret what the problem really is."

Mr. Lucky continued, "Belief number three is keeping you from recognizing your problem. Now think to yourself, what caused this problem?"

Utor didn't want to say what he was thinking, because it was too embarrassing now that his mind has been opened to new opportunities. He languished a little as he admitted, "I am clumsy, not very funny, and I let kids push me around."

"Okay," said Mr. Lucky, "Now you have found the real problem. Do you understand how I know this is the real problem?"

"No," said Utor.

Mr. Lucky explained, "When you said

'nobody likes me' that put the responsibility for your problem on the other kids to like you. When you said, 'I am clumsy and I let kids push me around' that is when you took responsibility for your own problem. Now that we know what the real problem is, what can we do about it?"

Utor thought for a moment then began speaking, "Well I could practice more in sports, read some —"

"No!" interrupted Mr. Lucky. "Now you went right to number one on the Mistaken Beliefs list. You don't necessarily have to solve your own problem. You need to move to step number two of Resource Masterminding. You have determined what the problem really is, according to step number one. Now you need to discover what resources are available to help you work on the problem."

"Well, what kind of resources could I use for this?" asked Utor.

Mr. Lucky replied, "What about teachers, family, books, sports equipment, friends, personal trainers, comedians, hobbies."

Just then Utor said, "I could never afford a personal trainer and—"

Mr. Lucky interrupted, "No, Utor, don't ever limit your resources, because it is in your resources where you will find your opportunities. You may even need to find resources for your resources. If your resource is a personal trainer and you have no money to pay for one, then you would also find a resource for money. In any case, list all the resources you can think of that, in a perfect situation, would exist for you."

Utor began thinking and then said sarcastically, "Okay then, how about my own personal bully?" Utor was shocked when Mr. Lucky wrote 'personal bully' on the board then said, "Next."

"I was only kidding," said Utor.

"Be that as it may, Utor, a personal bully

could prove useful, and I am not going to limit the resources."

Utor then realized that when it comes to seeking resources, Mr. Lucky intended to be very open minded. He thought to himself, "Wow, I guess you really can use anything available, or maybe even unavailable, to help in this Resource Masterminding." Now the wheels really started to turn in Utor's mind, and he began to give Mr. Lucky an extensive list of resources.

Mr. Lucky then said, "It is time to move on to step three. We need to give each of these resources a value from one to five, with five being the most likely to aid in serving our cause." Once they finished assigning values to the resources Mr. Lucky said, "In business it is always a good practice to sell off your bottom 20 percent performers so you can spend the resources targeted for that lower 20 percent on better performers. Therefore, we are going to erase all resources with a value of one."

Once they finished, it was time to move on to step number four. Without going into all the masterminding details, which took them more than an hour, they came up with the following opportunity:

Utor was going to exercise every day with Mr. Lucky's friend. The conditioning would build Utor's confidence and skill. Utor was also going to write his first book called *Finding Friends in the Briar Patch*. That would prepare him for the real book he would one day write with his newfound knowledge from Mr. Lucky. It was decided that Utor didn't care if he was funny, and learning comedy wasn't very interesting to him. However, Mr. Lucky remarked that Utor had exhibited an ability to be cynical, which is often considered funny, but he recommended Utor not use it too often because cynicism usually hurts feelings and causes people to avoid you.

Mr. Lucky erased the board and began to write down a list of potential opportunity resources. This list helped Utor to realize what was really available to him. The list consisted of, but was not limited to the following:

Books	Friends	Professionals	Brochures
Family	Materials	Animals	Food
Candy	Money	Plants	Incentives
Computers	Associations	Government	Clothing
Tools	Transportation	Utilities	Medicine
Fixtures	Manufacturers	Videos	Focus Groups
Radio	Media	Advisors	Postal Services
Consultants	Printers	Athletes	Rental Companies
Celebrities	Investors	Tapes	Fabricators
Internet	Maps	Magazines	Science
Artistry	Chemistry	News	Seminars
Pamphlets	Counselors	Church	Resource Centers
Guides	Surveys	Libraries	Business Networks
Teachers	Natural Resources	Statistics	Events

"The list does not end there, Utor," said Mr. Lucky. "Anything and anyone can be a resource. It is your ability to put resources together that will determine the synergy's effectiveness. That synergy will work for you in turning your problem into a successful opportunity. With a good plan for opportunity, derived from Resource Masterminding, it is almost impossible to fail," said Mr. Lucky.

Mr. Lucky ended by saying, "Utor, it is now time for you to go out and practice Resource Masterminding until you perfect it. On your new quest, you will make new discoveries. I will be interested in hearing of your discoveries and successes, but for now your training is over. You will make mistakes, Utor, but the more you practice and teach Resource Masterminding, the more you will perfect it.

"I have wanted so desperately to teach this principle to others, but it seems my name tends to be an obstacle. When someone asks my name and I reply 'I. M. Lucky,' he or she will immediately make judgments that I am privileged and therefore, he or she could never accomplish what I have. After a few attempts at teaching this principle, I realized I couldn't be the one to train people because of their mis-perceptions of me personally. That's when I started pondering on how I could give this principle to the world. My solution was to find someone else to write about it. That is when you came into the picture. I realized that once you learned how to find opportunity in the midst of any problem, you would be the opportunity in my problem. You will be the one to use this system to become even richer and more successful than I."

Utor excitedly said, "Yeah, then the day will come when everyone will call me Mr. I. M. Lucky."

"Not quite," said Mr. Lucky, "One day, Utor Retting, people will call you 'Lucky,' but you will be referred to as 'U. R. Lucky.' Do you see how ideal this really is? Now every time people ask your name and you reply, 'U. R. Lucky,' they will feel a sense of opportunity. They will realize they can be lucky just like you. You keep telling them 'U. R. Lucky,' and you will be the means of amassing even greater amounts of wealth than I, because you will not be doing it only for you, but you will do it for everyone who meets you. 'U. R. Lucky' will be the name everyone will go to for opportunity."

Mr. Lucky escorted Utor to the door, and as he was leaving Mr. Lucky said, "I will be anxiously awaiting the return of Mr. U. R. Lucky." This time, when Utor heard Mr. Lucky say, "U. R. Lucky," his heart and mind overflowed with courage, confidence, and determination.

Utor wrote his article for the school news-paper and, because of his newfound celebrity status obtained from the personal training of Mr. Lucky, everyone wanted to be his friend and learn the secrets of wealth possessed by Mr. Lucky. Utor's book was a success and he succeeded again and again until he could, from firsthand experience, write his book on Resource Masterminding. The people of Dilemmaville gave Utor's book to everyone in the town and made the practice of Resource Masterminding part of their regular routine.

A few years passed and the village of Dilemmaville changed its name to the City of Opportunity, at the behest of the now renowned Mr. U. R. Lucky.

As would be expected, the City of Opportunity became the wealthiest city in the country.

Speaker

If you would like to have Scott Taylor come to your company, business, association, or special event to teach you the art of turning problems into opportunities, call (435) 574-4800 or e-mail INFO@SAMARITANWAY.COM for availability and pricing.

Scott Taylor can also provide an entertaining training message in the areas of discovering *The Opportunity In Every Problem*, sales, marketing, brainstorming, customer care, management, motivation, business ethics, or doing business "The Samaritan Way."

Share Your Experience

It is our hope that you will use the inspiration you just received to turn your problems into opportunities. As you do, please send your stories to us for possible use in future books, seminars, or tapes. Your story may be the source of motivation needed to inspire some other individual to succeed. Please let us know how this book has inspired you. Send your stories via email to Info@SamaritanWay.com.

About the Author

Scott Taylor has spent most of his business life in marketing, sales, and business ownership. He has made significant changes to the profitability of small businesses where he has managed sales, international distribution, marketing, and tradeshows. He is a trainer of sales, marketing, and customer service courses. Scott created and organized the Samaritan Business Builders program where several of its members have learned to more than double their revenues in less than a year by doing business "The Samaritan Way."

Born and raised in California, Scott has been married for 17 years, has three children, and enjoys all sports and the arts. He lives in a secluded town of 400 people high in a beautiful mountain vista in a house he designed and built himself.